I0429931

101 Passive Income Ideas: Unlocking Financial Freedom

Copyright © 2024 by Evan J. Prospero

Table of Contents

Introduction

Embracing the Power of Passive Income

Welcome to "101 Passive Income Ideas: Unlocking Financial Freedom," a comprehensive guide designed to help you navigate the vast landscape of income-generating opportunities beyond the traditional 9-to-5 job. I'm Evan J. Prospero, your guide on this journey towards financial independence and flexibility. With a background in Finance and Economics from Stanford University, and years of experience as a financial advisor and entrepreneur, I have witnessed firsthand the transformative power of passive income in achieving personal and financial freedom.

The concept of earning money while you sleep may sound like a dream to many, but it's a reality for those who strategically build and diversify their income streams. The journey to establishing a passive income is not about getting rich quickly. Instead, it's about making calculated decisions and investments that pay off over time, providing financial security and the freedom to live life on your own terms.

The Inspiration Behind This Book

Throughout my career, I've encountered countless individuals feeling trapped in endless cycles of paycheck-to-paycheck living, despite their hard work and dedication. The common thread among them was not a lack of effort but a lack of knowledge about the opportunities available to generate income passively. This realization ignited my passion for sharing knowledge and empowering others to break free from financial constraints.

"101 Passive Income Ideas: Unlocking Financial Freedom" is born out of this passion. It's a distillation of years of research, experimentation, and conversations with successful investors, entrepreneurs, and financial experts. This book is designed to be your roadmap to understanding and leveraging passive income streams to build wealth and achieve financial independence.

How to Use This Book

This book is structured to guide you through the myriad of passive income opportunities available today, from online ventures to real estate investments and beyond. Each chapter delves into different categories of passive income, providing detailed insights, step-by-step instructions, and real-world examples to help you navigate and select the best options for your financial goals and lifestyle.

To get the most out of this book, I encourage you to approach it with an open mind and a willingness to explore new ideas. Passive income is not a one-size-fits-all solution; what works for one person may not work for another. Thus, consider your interests, skills, and resources as you explore each idea. Take notes, highlight sections that resonate with you, and don't be afraid to deep dive into further research or seek advice on specific opportunities that pique your interest.

A Journey to Financial Freedom

Embarking on the journey to building passive income is both exciting and challenging. It requires patience, persistence, and a proactive mindset. However, the rewards—financial freedom, increased flexibility, and the ability to live life on your own terms—are immeasurable.

As you turn the pages of this book, remember that every step you take towards building passive income streams is a step closer to unlocking a life of financial freedom. Whether you're looking to supplement your existing income, transition away from traditional employment, or build a diverse portfolio of income-generating assets, "101 Passive Income Ideas: Unlocking Financial Freedom" is here to guide you every step of the way.

Let's venturing on this journey together.

Evan J. Prospero

Chapter 1: Understanding Passive Income

The allure of earning money while you sleep is a concept that has captivated the imagination of countless individuals striving for financial independence. Passive income, as this phenomenon is known, stands as a cornerstone in the architecture of wealth-building, offering a pathway to financial freedom that diverges from the traditional earn-and-spend cycle. This chapter delves into the foundational aspects of passive income, laying the groundwork for a journey towards achieving financial autonomy.

Defining Passive Income

Passive income is often misconstrued as money that requires no effort to earn. However, a more accurate definition acknowledges the upfront time, effort, and sometimes capital investment, followed by minimal ongoing effort. Essentially, passive income streams generate revenue on a recurring basis from work done once. Examples span from rental income and dividends to earnings from a blog or a book.

Understanding the distinction between passive and active income is crucial. Active income, the antithesis of passive income, is what one earns from a job or business where direct involvement and time are traded for money. The salient feature of passive income lies in its ability to decouple earnings from time, offering scalability that active income seldom provides.

The Benefits of Passive Income

The benefits of cultivating passive income are manifold. **Firstly, it affords financial security and independence,** liberating individuals from the constraints of paycheck dependency. This financial cushion enables risk-taking and investment in opportunities that might otherwise be deemed too perilous.

Secondly, passive income offers the luxury of time. By generating income autonomously, individuals reclaim their time, allowing for pursuits of personal passions, hobbies, or further wealth-building ventures. This shift from trading time for money to leveraging time is a key milestone on the path to financial freedom.

Additionally, passive income contributes to wealth accumulation and longevity. It not only facilitates the attainment of financial goals but also ensures a sustained income stream that can support individuals during retirement, acting as a financial safety net that grows over time.

Challenges and Considerations

While the allure of passive income is undeniable, the path to creating successful passive income streams is fraught with challenges. **Initial capital outlay** is often required, whether in the form of monetary investment, such as purchasing real estate, or time investment, such as developing a blog. This upfront cost can be a barrier to entry for some.

Risk management is another critical consideration. Not all passive income ventures guarantee success, and some may even result in financial loss. Therefore, conducting thorough research, understanding market dynamics, and sometimes enduring trial and error are integral to identifying and mitigating risks associated with passive income investments.

Sustainability and scalability also pose significant challenges. Creating a passive income stream that not only generates consistent revenue but can also be scaled to increase earnings over time requires strategic planning and ongoing management. This might involve staying abreast of market trends, investing in maintenance, or updating content to remain relevant and competitive.

Despite these challenges, the pursuit of passive income remains a worthwhile endeavor for those committed to achieving financial independence. The key to success lies in diligent planning, informed decision-making, and a willingness to learn from both successes and setbacks.

Transitioning to Passive Income

For many, the transition from active to passive income involves a paradigm shift in how they perceive money and time. **Shifting from a mindset of earning money through direct labor to generating income passively** requires a strategic approach and, often, a period of overlap where both active and passive income streams coexist.

Starting small and scaling over time is a practical strategy for those new to passive income. This approach allows for learning and adjustment without the pressure of immediate financial dependence on these new income streams. Moreover, it provides an opportunity to experiment with different passive income ideas to discover what works best for an individual's skills, interests, and resources.

Educating oneself on financial literacy and investment strategies is another crucial step in the transition. Understanding the principles of investment, the power of compounding interest, and the importance of diversification can significantly enhance the effectiveness of passive income strategies.

Networking and seeking mentorship can also accelerate the journey towards successful passive income generation. Learning from those who have successfully navigated the path can provide invaluable insights and shortcuts to avoid common pitfalls and capitalize on proven strategies.

As we delve deeper into the various avenues for generating passive income in the subsequent chapters, it's important to remember that the foundation of any successful venture lies in a clear understanding of the principles outlined in this chapter. Armed with this knowledge, readers are better prepared to explore the myriad of opportunities that passive income presents, equipped to make informed decisions that align with their financial goals and lifestyle aspirations.

In summary, passive income represents a powerful tool in the quest for financial freedom, offering benefits that extend beyond mere monetary gain. Despite the challenges inherent in creating and sustaining passive income streams, the rewards—financial security, time freedom, and the capacity for wealth accumulation—are undeniably compelling. As we proceed, keep in mind the foundational concepts introduced here, as they will serve as guiding principles in your exploration of passive income opportunities.

Chapter 2: Online Passive Income Ideas

In today's digital age, the internet has become a fertile ground for generating passive income. With the right strategies, you can build income streams that flow into your bank account even while you sleep. This chapter explores five lucrative online passive income ideas, providing you with a roadmap to financial independence through digital means.

Blogging

Blogging stands as one of the most popular methods for earning passive income online. It allows you to express your passions, share expertise, and connect with a global audience. To start a profitable blog, follow these steps:

1. **Choose Your Niche**: Select a topic you are passionate about and that has a sizable audience interested in it. Niches like personal finance, health and fitness, and technology are evergreen options with broad appeal.

2. **Set Up Your Blog**: Choose a blogging platform like WordPress and select a hosting provider. Customize your blog's design to reflect your niche and personality.

3. **Create Compelling Content**: Consistently publish high-quality, valuable content that solves problems or entertains your target audience. Use SEO techniques to improve your visibility on search engines.

4. **Monetize Your Blog**: Implement monetization strategies such as displaying ads, affiliate marketing, selling digital products, or offering memberships for exclusive content.

5. **Drive Traffic**: Utilize social media, email marketing, and networking with other bloggers to increase your blog's traffic.

Affiliate Marketing

Affiliate marketing is an excellent way to earn income by promoting other people's products and earning a commission for every sale made through your referral. Here's how to succeed in affiliate marketing:

1. **Choose the Right Products**: Select products that align with your audience's interests and your content. Look for high-quality products with a good commission structure.

2. **Find Affiliate Programs**: Join affiliate programs through networks like Amazon Associates, ClickBank, or directly from companies offering affiliate programs.

3. **Promote Affiliate Products**: Use your blog, social media channels, or email newsletters to promote affiliate products. Create valuable content around the products to encourage purchases.

4. **Optimize for Conversions**: Use persuasive calls-to-action and track the performance of your affiliate links. Test different strategies to see what works best for your audience.

5. **Comply with Legal Requirements**: Disclose your affiliate relationships to your audience in accordance with FTC guidelines to maintain transparency and trust.

E-Commerce

Starting an e-commerce store is a powerful way to generate passive income by selling physical or digital products online. Here are the steps to launch a successful e-commerce store:

1. **Choose Your Business Model**: Decide whether you want to create your own products, dropship products from suppliers, or use print-on-demand services for custom merchandise.

2. **Select Your Platform**: Use e-commerce platforms like Shopify, WooCommerce, or Etsy to build your online store.

3. **Source Your Products**: For dropshipping, partner with reliable suppliers. If you're creating your own products, ensure you have a production and fulfillment strategy in place.

4. **Market Your Store**: Use social media marketing, search engine optimization, and email marketing to attract customers to your store.

5. **Automate and Scale**: As your store grows, automate order processing and customer service to maintain your passive income stream.

Digital Products

Selling digital products is a fantastic way to earn passive income because you create the product once and sell it repeatedly without replenishing inventory. Digital products can include e-books, courses, software, and templates.

1. **Create Your Product**: Identify a need or gap in your niche and create a digital product that addresses it. Ensure your product delivers value and is of high quality.

2. **Set Up a Sales Platform**: Use platforms like Gumroad, Teachable, or your own website to sell your digital products.

3. **Market Your Product**: Utilize your blog, social media, and email list to promote your product. Consider offering free samples or mini-courses to entice potential customers.

4. **Automate Sales and Delivery**: Set up an automated system for payments and product delivery to ensure a passive sales process.

5. **Gather Feedback and Iterate**: Use customer feedback to improve your product and create additional offerings.

Investing in Stocks and Dividends

Investing in dividend-paying stocks is a traditional method of generating passive income. By investing in the stock market, you can earn dividends regularly without actively managing your investments.

1. **Educate Yourself**: Learn the basics of the stock market and understand what makes a good dividend stock. Consider factors like the dividend yield, company stability, and growth potential.

2. **Open a Brokerage Account**: Choose a reputable online brokerage and open an account. Look for platforms with low fees and a good selection of dividend stocks.

3. **Select Your Stocks**: Diversify your portfolio by selecting stocks from different sectors and industries. Consider using dividend reinvestment plans (DRIPs) to automatically reinvest your dividends into additional shares.

4. **Monitor Your Portfolio**: Keep an eye on your investments and the market conditions, but remember that dividend investing is a long-term strategy.

5. **Reinvest Dividends**: Use your dividends to purchase additional shares, compounding your earnings and accelerating the growth of your investment portfolio.

By leveraging these online passive income ideas, you can build a diversified income stream that brings financial security and freedom. Each method has its unique advantages and challenges, but with dedication and the right strategies, you can achieve success in the digital world. Remember, the key to building a sustainable passive income is to start with one idea, master it, and then gradually expand your portfolio to include multiple streams of income.

Chapter 3: Real Estate for Passive Income

Real estate investment stands as a cornerstone of wealth building, offering a multitude of pathways to generate passive income. This chapter delves into the nuanced world of real estate, guiding you through the complexities and opportunities of rental properties, Real Estate Investment Trusts (REITs), and Airbnb and short-term rentals. Each section is designed to equip you with the knowledge and tools necessary to embark on your real estate investment journey, whether you're a seasoned investor or a novice looking to diversify your income streams.

Rental Properties: The Gateway to Real Estate Investing

Single-family Homes: Beginning your journey into real estate with single-family homes can be a straightforward entry point. These properties are often in high demand among renters, especially in suburban areas or cities with strong family-oriented communities. The key to success lies in meticulous market research, focusing on neighborhoods with low vacancy rates, strong school districts, and consistent property value appreciation. Financing these investments typically involves securing a mortgage, where a 20% down payment is standard, though various financing options exist to lower this barrier for new investors.

Multi-family Units: Investing in multi-family units, such as duplexes or apartment buildings, offers the advantage of multiple income streams from a single property. These properties can yield a higher rental income compared to single-family homes and potentially offer economies of scale in maintenance and management costs. However, they also require more significant initial capital and a deeper understanding of property management. Effective management of multi-family units involves balancing occupancy rates, managing tenant relations, and maintaining the property to ensure its long-term viability as an income source.

Vacation Rentals: The vacation rental market has exploded in popularity, thanks in part to platforms like Airbnb and VRBO. Properties in high-demand tourist destinations can offer substantial rental income, especially during peak seasons. Success in this niche requires a keen eye for properties with unique appeal or located in areas with year-round tourism. The operational aspect involves dynamic pricing strategies, exceptional guest communication, and creating memorable experiences to secure high ratings and repeat bookings.

Commercial Real Estate: For those looking to diversify beyond residential properties, commercial real estate presents an opportunity. This category includes office buildings, retail spaces, and warehouses. Commercial leases are typically longer than residential ones, offering more stability in cash flow. However, entering the commercial real estate market requires a more significant investment and understanding of commercial tenant needs, zoning laws, and market trends.

Rent-to-Own Properties: The rent-to-own strategy bridges the gap between renting and homeownership for tenants and can be a lucrative model for investors. In this arrangement, a portion of the rent goes towards a future down payment on the property purchase. For investors, this model offers regular rental income, with the potential for a property sale at the end of the lease term. It requires careful legal structuring to ensure clear terms and protect both parties' interests.

REITs: Real Estate Investment Without the Hassles of Property Management

Equity REITs: Equity REITs own and operate income-generating real estate. Investors can buy shares of these REITs, effectively becoming partial owners of a portfolio of properties. This type of REIT primarily earns income through leasing space and collecting rents on the properties they own, and then distributing that income to shareholders as dividends. Equity REITs offer exposure to a variety of property types, including commercial, residential, and industrial.

Mortgage REITs: Unlike equity REITs, mortgage REITs provide financing for income-producing real estate by purchasing or originating mortgages and mortgage-backed securities. They earn income from the interest on these financial assets. This type of REIT is more sensitive to changes in interest rates, so investors should consider the current economic environment when investing.

Hybrid REITs: Hybrid REITs combine the investment strategies of both equity and mortgage REITs, holding both properties and mortgages. This diversification can offer a balance between the potential for high income and the stability of owning physical assets, depending on the REIT's focus and management strategy.

Public Non-Listed REITs (PNLRs): PNLRs are registered with the SEC but do not trade on national securities exchanges. This type of REIT can offer diversification and potential for income but is typically less liquid than publicly traded REITs, making it a longer-term investment. Investors should be mindful of the fees associated with PNLRs, which can be higher than those of publicly traded REITs.

Private REITs: Private REITs are not registered with the SEC and do not trade on national securities exchanges. They are typically available only to accredited investors and offer exposure to real estate investments with potentially higher returns, albeit with higher risk and less liquidity. Due diligence is crucial when investing in private REITs, given their lack of regulatory oversight compared to public REITs.

Airbnb and Short-Term Rentals: Capitalizing on the Sharing Economy

Urban Apartments: Investing in urban apartments for short-term rentals can tap into the constant demand from business travelers and tourists seeking city experiences. Key to success is choosing locations with high foot traffic, proximity to major attractions, and easy access to public transportation. Operational excellence in managing bookings, maintaining high standards of hospitality, and leveraging technology for seamless guest experiences are essential.

Luxury Villas: The high-end segment of the short-term rental market can offer significant returns, targeting travelers willing to pay a premium for luxury accommodations. These properties must not only be in prime locations but also offer exceptional amenities and services. Marketing these properties requires high-quality photography, targeted advertising, and partnerships with luxury travel agents or concierge services.

Unique Accommodations: Treehouses, yurts, and other unique accommodations have carved a niche in the short-term rental market, appealing to travelers seeking unusual experiences. These properties often rely on their novelty factor and natural settings to attract bookings. Success in this niche requires creative marketing strategies, emphasizing the unique aspects and experiences offered.

Co-hosting: For those not ready to invest in property, co-hosting offers a way to enter the short-term rental market. Co-hosts manage properties on behalf of owners, handling listing, guest communication, and property maintenance. This arrangement allows for earning income from short-term rentals without owning real estate, developing skills in hospitality and property management.

Airbnb Experiences: Beyond renting out space, Airbnb Experiences allow hosts to offer guided tours, classes, and unique local experiences. This can be a supplementary income stream for Airbnb hosts or a standalone option for those with expertise in areas of interest to tourists. Successful experiences offer authenticity, personal connection, and access to activities or locations not easily found through traditional channels.

Real estate investment for passive income is a diverse field, offering opportunities across various markets and investment sizes. Whether through direct property investment, REITs, or innovative short-term rental models, real estate remains a powerful vehicle for building wealth. As you consider these options, remember that success in real estate requires research, due diligence, and sometimes, patience, as investments mature and yield returns. The journey into real estate investing can be both challenging and rewarding, opening doors to financial freedom and the ability to generate lasting passive income.

Chapter 4: Creative Passive Income Streams

Unlocking the potential of your creativity can be one of the most fulfilling ways to generate passive income. Whether you're an artist, a musician, a writer, or a developer, leveraging your talents can lead to substantial earnings over time. This chapter explores various avenues for artists, creators, and innovators to turn their intellectual property into a continuous income stream without the need for ongoing work.

Royalties from Intellectual Property

1. Book Royalties: Writing a book is a labor of love and a monumental task, but once published, it can provide you with a steady income. Whether you choose the traditional publishing route or decide to self-publish, each book sold generates royalties. The key to success in this realm is quality content, a good marketing strategy, and leveraging platforms like Amazon Kindle Direct Publishing to reach a wide audience.

2. Music Royalties: For the musically inclined, creating songs can lead to ongoing income through royalties. Platforms like

Spotify, Apple Music, and YouTube pay royalties to artists for streams and downloads. To maximize earnings, consider distributing your music through a digital distribution service that places your music on all major platforms. Additionally, registering with a Performing Rights Organization (PRO) ensures you collect royalties whenever your music is played in public venues.

3. Patent Licensing: Inventors can earn passive income by patenting their inventions and licensing the rights to companies. This strategy allows you to profit from your invention without bearing the cost of production or marketing. Licensing agreements can be structured to provide ongoing royalties based on sales, offering a potentially lucrative passive income stream.

4. Stock Photos: Photographers can generate passive income by selling their photos to stock photography websites like Shutterstock or Getty Images. Once uploaded, your photos can be sold repeatedly, earning you money each time they're downloaded. The key is to produce high-quality, in-demand images that appeal to a broad range of customers.

5. Software Licenses: If you're skilled in software development, creating an application or software tool can provide a continuous stream of income through sales or subscriptions. Offering your software under a licensing agreement means customers pay to use your product, generating ongoing revenue without additional work on your part.

Selling Photography and Art Online

1. Stock Photography Websites: Beyond selling photos, consider specializing in specific niches that are underrepresented. This can increase your visibility and sales potential on platforms like Adobe Stock or iStock.

2. Art Prints: Artists can sell prints of their original work online. Services like Society6 or Redbubble allow you to upload your artwork, which they print on a variety of items whenever a customer makes a purchase, from prints to merchandise like t-shirts and phone cases.

3. Merchandise with Your Designs: Platforms like Teespring and Merch by Amazon let you place your designs on apparel and other products, which are then sold on a print-on-demand basis. You create the designs; they handle the rest, from printing to shipping.

4. Digital Commissions: Offering custom digital artwork, such as portraits or logo designs, can attract clients interested in personalized work. Platforms like Etsy or Fiverr are great places to start, allowing you to reach a wide audience looking for custom creations.

5. NFTs (Non-Fungible Tokens): The digital art world has been revolutionized by NFTs, allowing creators to sell unique digital artwork for potentially high prices. By minting your work as an NFT, you ensure its authenticity and rarity, making it more valuable to collectors. Platforms like OpenSea or Rarible provide marketplaces for buying and selling NFTs.

YouTube and Content Creation

1. Ad Revenue: Monetizing your YouTube channel through ads can generate significant income. The key is creating engaging, high-quality content that attracts a large audience, increasing the number of views and, consequently, ad revenue.

2. Channel Memberships: Once you have a substantial following, offering channel memberships can provide a steady income. Members pay a monthly fee in exchange for exclusive perks, such as early access to videos or members-only content.

3. Super Chat: During live streams, viewers can purchase Super Chat messages to highlight their messages in the chat stream. It's a way for fans to support you while increasing their visibility during your live events.

4. Merchandise Shelf: YouTube allows creators to showcase their merchandise directly below their videos. This integration makes it easy for fans to purchase your branded merchandise, from t-shirts to stickers, directly from your YouTube channel.

5. Sponsored Content: Partnering with brands to create sponsored content can be highly lucrative. This involves promoting a brand's product or service in your videos for a fee. The key is to partner with brands that are relevant to your audience to maintain your channel's integrity and trust.

6. Patreon: Patreon is a platform that allows fans to support creators through monthly subscriptions. In return, patrons receive exclusive content or experiences. It's a way to monetize your audience's loyalty and engage with your most dedicated fans on a deeper level.

7. Educational Videos: Creating educational content, such as tutorials, courses, or how-to guides, can attract a dedicated audience. Platforms like Udemy or Teachable allow you to sell your courses, providing value to your audience while earning passive income.

8. Vlogs: Vlogging, or video blogging, can attract a wide audience by sharing your life, thoughts, or experiences. Successful vlogs often focus on engaging storytelling and relatable content, creating a loyal viewer base.

9. Gaming Channels: If you're passionate about gaming, creating a channel focused on video game playthroughs, reviews, or tips can attract fellow gamers. Engaging content and a unique personality can help you stand out in the crowded gaming niche.

10. DIY Tutorials: For the crafty and creative, DIY tutorial channels provide a platform to share your skills with an audience interested in learning. From home decor to sewing, engaging tutorials that provide value can build a substantial and dedicated audience.

Each of these creative passive income streams offers a unique way to monetize your talents and interests. The key to success lies in consistency, quality, and engagement with your audience. By diversifying your income sources and continually refining your approach, you can build a sustainable income that rewards your creative endeavors for years to come.

Chapter 5: Passive Income Through Business and Entrepreneurship

In the journey toward financial freedom, creating a business that can eventually run itself is the pinnacle of passive income. This chapter explores the nuances of starting a business with the potential for passive income, the art of automating and outsourcing, and the unique opportunities franchising offers. Let's dive into the practical steps and strategies that can set you on the path to building a business that not only thrives but also provides you with the freedom you seek.

Starting a Business with Passive Income Potential

Automated E-commerce

The allure of e-commerce lies in its scalability and the potential for automation. Starting an e-commerce business typically involves selecting a niche, sourcing products, and setting up an online store. The key to transitioning this into a passive income stream is automation. Tools like Shopify and WooCommerce can integrate with third-party fulfillment services, automating inventory management, order processing, and shipping. By also employing email marketing automation and using AI for customer service (like chatbots), you can significantly reduce the daily operational workload.

Content Websites

Content websites, or niche blogs, monetize through advertising, affiliate marketing, and digital product sales. The initial phase requires heavy lifting: researching a niche, creating valuable content, and driving traffic. However, with a focus on evergreen content and SEO, these sites can attract visitors and generate income long-term. Using content management systems like WordPress, coupled with SEO tools and automated social media marketing, can help maintain and grow the site with minimal ongoing effort.

Niche Subscription Services

Subscription models provide consistent, recurring revenue. Whether it's curated boxes of goods, access to premium content, or software as a service (SaaS), subscriptions can be incredibly lucrative. The key is identifying a niche market with specific needs or interests. For physical goods, partnering with fulfillment centers can automate the packing and shipping process. For digital services, leveraging cloud-based platforms allows for scalability and reliability with little need for day-to-day management.

SEO Businesses

An SEO business focuses on helping other businesses improve their online visibility. While it requires expertise in SEO strategies, much of the work, from keyword research to content creation, can be automated or outsourced. Tools like SEMrush or Ahrefs automate analysis and reporting, while freelance writers and backlink services can help scale content and link-building efforts. With a solid client base, this can become a source of recurring revenue.

Social Media Management

Many companies seek to outsource their social media presence. Starting a social media management business involves creating and curating content, scheduling posts, and engaging with followers. By using social media management tools like Buffer or Hootsuite, you can automate much of the process. As your client base grows, you can hire freelancers or use AI-driven content creation tools to maintain scalability, turning your operation into a largely passive business.

Automating and Outsourcing

The transition from active management to passive income in business often hinges on the ability to automate processes and outsource tasks effectively.

Virtual Assistant Agencies

Virtual assistants (VAs) can handle a wide array of tasks, from email management to scheduling and social media. By starting a VA agency, you can connect VAs with businesses in need. The agency's role becomes one of management and matchmaking, which can be streamlined with the right software, automating client-VA matchups and billing.

Drop Servicing

Drop servicing involves selling services, like graphic design or writing, and then outsourcing the work to freelancers. Your focus is on marketing and customer service, acting as the middleman. Platforms like Upwork and Fiverr make finding quality freelancers easier, while project management tools can automate workflows and communication.

Automated Marketing Services

Digital marketing services, particularly those that can be automated like email marketing campaigns or PPC advertising, offer a scalable business model. By using software that automates campaign creation, analytics, and reporting, you can offer clients valuable services with minimal manual intervention.

Outsourced Client Services

Many businesses, especially in the tech industry, outsource their customer service departments. Starting a business that provides outsourced customer service involves setting up a team of remote customer service representatives. With advances in AI and machine learning, integrating chatbots for basic inquiries can further reduce the workload and improve efficiency.

Automated Sales Funnels

An automated sales funnel is a sequence of marketing messages designed to guide a potential customer through the buying process. Tools like ClickFunnels or Leadpages allow entrepreneurs to set up these sequences once and then let them run, automatically moving leads towards sales with minimal ongoing input.

Franchising

Franchising offers a unique blend of entrepreneurship and passive income. By investing in a franchise, you're buying into a proven business model and brand, which can reduce the risk and effort involved in starting a business from scratch.

Fast-food Franchises

Fast-food franchises are among the most recognizable forms of franchising. They offer standardized operations, which means once you've set up your franchise and trained your staff, much of the day-to-day operations can be managed by your team, allowing you to step back.

Retail Franchises

Retail franchises operate on a similar principle, providing a mix of brand recognition and operational support. Success in retail franchising often comes down to location and local marketing, which can be managed with a well-trained staff and corporate support.

Service-based Franchises

These franchises provide a service, such as cleaning, landscaping, or automotive repair. The franchisor typically offers training, operational guidelines, and marketing support, making it easier to run the business passively by hiring managers and staff to perform the daily work.

Home-based Franchises

Home-based franchises are appealing for their low overhead and flexibility. Many of these businesses, like travel planning or tutoring services, can be operated with just a computer and phone, making it easier to automate and outsource tasks.

Fitness Franchises

The fitness industry has seen a surge in franchising, from gyms to specialized classes like yoga or Pilates. These franchises benefit from brand recognition and operational systems provided by the franchisor, allowing for easier management and potential for passive income through membership fees.

Starting and running a business with the aim of generating passive income is a challenge that requires foresight, strategy, and a willingness to delegate and automate. By carefully selecting your business model, leveraging technology, and building a reliable team, you can create a business that not only supports your financial goals but also affords you the lifestyle you desire. Whether it's through innovative online ventures, the strategic use of automation and outsourcing, or the unique opportunities presented by franchising, the path to creating a passive income business is varied and rich with potential. Remember, the goal is to work smarter, not harder, allowing you to enjoy the fruits of your labor without being tied down by day-to-day operations.

Chapter 6: Financial Products and Investments

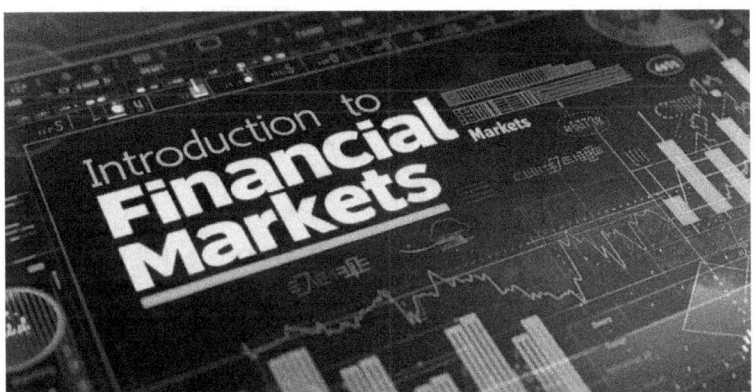

In the world of passive income, diversifying your portfolio is not just a strategy; it's a necessity. The financial markets offer a plethora of opportunities to invest your capital and watch it grow without the active involvement that traditional income streams demand. This chapter delves into the nuanced world of financial products and investments, breaking down complex concepts into actionable insights. From the collaborative potential of peer-to-peer lending to the steady returns of annuities and the exciting possibilities of crowdfunding and venture capital, we explore 15 distinct avenues that can bolster your passive income portfolio and spread your risk across multiple assets.

Peer-to-Peer Lending

1. Consumer Loans: These are unsecured loans provided to individuals for personal, family, or household purposes. By investing in consumer loans through peer-to-peer (P2P) platforms, you can earn interest as borrowers repay their loans. It's akin to playing the role of a bank, but with the ability to choose whom you lend to and at what rates.

2. Business Loans: Small and medium-sized enterprises (SMEs) often seek alternative financing options outside of traditional banking systems. P2P platforms facilitate business loans, allowing investors to fund burgeoning enterprises in exchange for attractive interest rates. This not only diversifies your investment portfolio but also supports the growth of the business sector.

3. Real Estate Loans: These loans are secured by real estate properties. Investors can contribute to loans for residential or commercial real estate projects on P2P platforms. The appeal lies in the security of having a tangible asset as collateral, which potentially lowers the risk compared to unsecured loans.

4. Student Loans: Investing in student loans is a way to support learners while earning income from the interest paid over the life of the loan. P2P lending platforms offer opportunities to fund student loans, providing a financial lifeline to students and returns to investors.

5. Green Loans: These are loans specifically intended for funding eco-friendly and sustainable projects. By investing in green loans, you're not only earning passive income but also contributing to environmental sustainability. This segment is growing as more borrowers look for ways to finance renewable energy projects, green buildings, and sustainable agriculture.

Annuities and Insurance Products

6. Fixed Annuities: A fixed annuity is an insurance product that provides a guaranteed interest rate on your investment. You pay a lump sum upfront, and the insurance company pays you a steady income for a predetermined period or for life. This is a conservative investment, ideal for those seeking stability in their passive income streams.

7. Variable Annuities: Unlike fixed annuities, variable annuities allow you to invest in various securities, such as mutual funds. Your payouts depend on the performance of these investments.

While they offer higher potential returns, they also come with greater risk and complexity.

8. Indexed Annuities: These are a hybrid between fixed and variable annuities. Your returns are linked to a market index, like the S&P 500, but you have a guaranteed minimum return. This means you can benefit from market upswings while being protected against downturns, making it a balanced option for risk-averse investors.

9. Life Insurance Cash Value: Permanent life insurance policies, such as whole life and universal life, include a cash value component that grows over time. Policyholders can borrow against this cash value or even withdraw it during their lifetime, offering a unique way to generate passive income while also providing life insurance coverage.

10. Long-Term Care Annuities: These specialized annuities are designed to help cover long-term care expenses, such as home care or assisted living. By investing in a long-term care annuity, you're ensuring that you have a dedicated source of income to cover these costs if needed, providing peace of mind and financial security.

Crowdfunding and Venture Capital

11. Equity Crowdfunding: This allows individuals to invest small amounts of money in startups in exchange for equity. Platforms that offer equity crowdfunding enable you to diversify your investments across various industries and stages of business growth. While risky, the potential for significant returns if a company succeeds is a compelling draw.

12. Real Estate Crowdfunding: Similar to equity crowdfunding, but specifically focused on real estate investments. Investors can put their money into commercial or residential properties and earn returns based on rental income and property appreciation. This is an accessible way to enter the real estate market without the need for substantial upfront capital.

13. Peer-to-Peer Lending Platforms: While traditionally associated with loans, some P2P platforms also allow for equity investments in businesses. This merges the concept of lending with the potential for equity growth, offering a unique blend of fixed income and growth potential.

14. Angel Investing: Angel investors provide capital to startups in exchange for ownership equity or convertible debt. While traditionally the domain of the wealthy, various platforms now allow smaller investors to participate in angel investing, democratizing access to early-stage investment opportunities.

15. Venture Capital Funds: These funds pool money from various investors to invest in high-growth startups. By investing in a venture capital fund, you gain exposure to a diversified portfolio of emerging companies with the potential for high returns. It's a way to engage in the high-stakes world of startup investing, but with a layer of professional management to mitigate risk.

Building a Robust Portfolio

The art of constructing a passive income portfolio lies in balancing risk and reward. Financial products and investments offer a spectrum of opportunities, from the steady predictability of annuities to the dynamic potential of equity crowdfunding and venture capital. As you explore these avenues, consider your financial goals, risk tolerance, and the time horizon over which you expect to see returns.

Peer-to-Peer Lending: A Closer Look

Peer-to-peer lending has revolutionized the way individuals and businesses access financing. By acting as a lender on P2P platforms, you can achieve attractive returns, but it's essential to conduct thorough due diligence. Diversifying across different types of loans and borrowers can mitigate risk. Remember, while higher interest rates can be tempting, they also reflect higher risk.

Annuities and Insurance Products: Security and Returns

Annuities offer a sense of security with their predictable income, making them a cornerstone for many passive income portfolios. However, it's crucial to understand the fees associated with these products and how they impact your potential returns. Consulting with a financial advisor can help you navigate these complexities and ensure that these products align with your overall investment strategy.

Crowdfunding and Venture Capital: High Risk, High Reward

Investing in startups through crowdfunding or venture capital can be exhilarating, offering a front-row seat to innovation and the potential for substantial returns. However, the high risk of failure in startups cannot be overstated. Spreading your investments across different companies and sectors can help manage this risk, but it's vital to only invest what you can afford to lose in this volatile space.

A Note on Diversification

Diversification is more than just a buzzword; it's your best defense against the unpredictability of the market. By spreading your investments across different financial products and asset classes, you can reduce the impact of any single investment's poor performance on your overall portfolio. This chapter provides a roadmap to building a diversified portfolio that aligns with your financial goals and risk tolerance.

Monitoring Your Investments

Active monitoring is a critical component of managing your passive income investments. Regularly reviewing your portfolio's performance allows you to make informed decisions about rebalancing or adjusting your investment strategy. Tools and platforms are available to help track your investments, offering insights into performance metrics and trends that can inform your decisions.

The Future of Passive Income Investments

The landscape of passive income investments is ever-evolving, with new opportunities emerging as financial technologies and markets develop. Staying informed about these changes and being willing to adapt your strategy accordingly can position you to take advantage of new avenues for growth and income.

As we delve deeper into each category of financial products and investments, remember that the journey to building a robust passive income stream is a marathon, not a sprint. Patience, diligence, and a willingness to learn from the market's ebbs and flows will serve you well on this journey.

Chapter 7: Creating a Passive Income Portfolio

In the quest for financial freedom, diversification is not just a strategy; it's a necessity. This chapter delves into the art and science of building a passive income portfolio that not only withstands market volatility but thrives in it. By carefully selecting a mix of passive income streams, you can create a robust financial safety net that grows over time, ensuring a steady flow of income from multiple sources. Here, we'll guide you through the process of combining the diverse passive income ideas discussed in previous chapters into a cohesive portfolio that aligns with your financial goals, risk tolerance, and time horizon.

The Foundation of Your Portfolio

Begin with a solid foundation, focusing on income streams that offer stability and reliability. Rental properties and dividend-paying stocks are cornerstone assets in this category. These investments have historically provided consistent returns and can serve as a buffer during economic downturns. When selecting rental properties, consider factors such as location, market demand, and the potential for appreciation. For dividend stocks, look for companies with a strong track record of paying dividends and the potential for capital growth.

Adding Layers of Growth

With your foundation in place, it's time to layer in investments that offer higher growth potential. This is where you can incorporate real estate investment trusts (REITs), peer-to-peer lending, and crowdfunded ventures. REITs allow you to invest in real estate sectors without the need to directly manage properties, offering liquidity and diversity. Peer-to-peer lending can provide higher returns than traditional savings accounts, albeit with increased risk. Crowdfunding ventures offer the opportunity to be part of early-stage investments, which, while risky, can yield significant returns if the business succeeds.

Sprinkling in High-Risk, High-Reward Options

For those willing to accept higher levels of risk for the potential of higher rewards, consider adding speculative investments to your portfolio. This could include cryptocurrency, NFTs, or investing in startups through venture capital funds or angel investing. These options should represent a smaller portion of your portfolio due to their volatile nature. However, they can provide substantial returns that significantly boost your overall portfolio performance. It's crucial to conduct thorough research and only invest funds you can afford to lose in this category.

Automating and Outsourcing

To truly make your income passive, automation and outsourcing are key. For your online business ventures, such as e-commerce stores or blogs, leverage tools and software that automate daily operations. Consider outsourcing tasks like content creation, customer service, and order fulfillment to focus on strategic growth. In real estate, property management companies can handle day-to-day operations, allowing you to earn rental income without the hassle of direct management.

Regular Monitoring and Rebalancing

Creating a passive income portfolio is not a set-it-and-forget-it endeavor. Regular monitoring and rebalancing are essential to ensure your portfolio aligns with your evolving financial goals and market conditions. Set a schedule to review your portfolio's performance at least annually. This review should assess each income stream's profitability, the overall balance of your portfolio, and whether any adjustments are needed to maintain your desired level of risk exposure.

Diversification Across Industries and Geographies

Diversification extends beyond just having multiple income streams; it also means spreading your investments across different industries and geographies. This strategy reduces the risk of significant losses if one sector or region faces a downturn. For example, your real estate investments could include properties in both residential and commercial sectors, spread across various cities or even countries. Similarly, your stock investments can include a mix of sectors such as technology, healthcare, and consumer goods, and span across global markets.

Leveraging Tax-Advantaged Accounts

To maximize your passive income, consider leveraging tax-advantaged accounts such as IRAs or 401(k)s for your stock and REIT investments. These accounts can offer tax-free growth or deferred taxes on dividends and capital gains, enhancing your overall returns. Be sure to understand the contribution limits and withdrawal rules associated with these accounts to optimize your tax benefits.

Risk Management Strategies

Risk management is crucial in safeguarding your passive income streams. This includes having an emergency fund to cover unexpected expenses or income fluctuations. Additionally, consider using insurance products, such as landlord insurance for rental properties or business insurance for your entrepreneurial ventures, to protect against potential losses. Diversifying your investment types and sectors also plays a key role in risk management, helping to ensure that a downturn in one area doesn't disproportionately impact your entire portfolio.

The Role of Patience and Persistence

Patience and persistence are virtues in the journey toward building a successful passive income portfolio. Some investments may take time to start generating significant returns, while others may face temporary setbacks. Stay committed to your long-term financial goals, and resist the temptation to make impulsive decisions based on short-term market fluctuations. Remember, the goal is to build a portfolio that provides financial security and grows over time.

Staying Informed and Adapting to Change

The financial landscape is constantly evolving, with new investment opportunities emerging and market conditions changing. Staying informed about economic trends and new passive income strategies is key to adapting your portfolio to capitalize on new opportunities and navigate challenges. Regularly educate yourself through financial news, investment books, and online courses. Engaging with a financial advisor or joining investment communities can also provide valuable insights and support as you refine your passive income strategies.

Building a Legacy

Beyond achieving financial freedom for yourself, consider how your passive income portfolio can contribute to building a legacy for your family. This could involve setting up trust funds, investing in education savings accounts, or teaching your children about financial management and investing. By planning for the future, you can ensure that your passive income streams have a lasting impact, providing security and opportunities for generations to come.

In building a diversified passive income portfolio, you're not just creating multiple streams of income; you're constructing a financial ecosystem that can support your lifestyle, fulfill your long-term goals, and provide security for the unforeseen. The journey requires diligence, strategic planning, and a mindset geared towards growth and adaptation. While the path to developing a robust passive income portfolio is unique for each individual, the principles outlined in this chapter provide a roadmap for anyone aiming to achieve financial independence through passive income.

Chapter 8: Tips for Success and Common Pitfalls

In the journey to create and sustain passive income streams, the path is often fraught with both opportunities and obstacles. Understanding how to navigate these waters is crucial for anyone looking to build their financial independence through passive income. This chapter delves into the essential tips for success and highlights common pitfalls to avoid, drawing on the collective wisdom of seasoned investors and entrepreneurs. By adhering to these guidelines, you can enhance your chances of achieving your financial goals while minimizing risks.

Building and Maintaining Motivation

Stay Focused on Your Goals: It's easy to get sidetracked or overwhelmed by the array of options and challenges that come with establishing passive income streams. To maintain your focus, keep a clear vision of your financial goals. Whether it's achieving financial independence, saving for retirement, or simply generating extra income, remind yourself regularly of why you started this journey. Setting short-term, achievable objectives alongside your long-term goals can also help maintain momentum and motivation.

Learning from Success and Failure: Embrace both your successes and failures as learning opportunities. Analyze what worked well and why, and more importantly, understand the reasons behind your setbacks. This reflective process is invaluable for refining your strategies and avoiding similar pitfalls in the future.

Building a Support Network: Surround yourself with a community of like-minded individuals who are also pursuing passive income. This network can provide support, advice, and encouragement, as well as opportunities for collaboration. Online forums, social media groups, and local meetups can be great places to connect with others on a similar path.

Scaling and Growing Your Income

Reinvest Your Profits: One of the keys to growing your passive income is to reinvest your earnings. By funneling profits back into your investments or using them to launch new income streams, you compound your ability to generate wealth. This approach requires discipline, as it can be tempting to spend your earnings, but the long-term benefits are well worth the sacrifice.

Diversify Your Portfolio: Don't put all your eggs in one basket. Diversification is a fundamental principle of investing that applies equally to passive income. By spreading your investments across different assets and income streams, you reduce risk and increase the likelihood of consistent returns. If one venture falters, others can sustain your overall portfolio.

Stay Informed and Adapt: The world of passive income is dynamic, with new opportunities and challenges emerging constantly. Stay informed about trends in your chosen areas, whether it's real estate, the stock market, e-commerce, or any other domain. Be ready to adapt your strategies in response to changing market conditions and technological advancements.

Avoiding Common Pitfalls

Overlooking Due Diligence: Enthusiasm for a new passive income opportunity can sometimes lead to hasty decisions without proper research. Always conduct thorough due diligence before committing your time or money. This includes analyzing market trends, understanding the competitive landscape, and assessing the potential risks and returns of your investment.

Underestimating the Initial Effort: Many passive income streams require significant upfront effort to set up. Underestimating the time, energy, and resources needed can lead to frustration and burnout. Be realistic about the initial workload and prepare accordingly, ensuring you have the necessary resources at your disposal.

Ignoring Legal and Tax Implications: Each passive income stream comes with its own set of legal and tax considerations. Failing to address these can lead to costly penalties and undermine your earnings. Consult with professionals to ensure you're compliant with laws and regulations, and that you're optimizing your tax strategy.

Falling for Scams and Get-Rich-Quick Schemes: The allure of quick and easy money can be tempting, but it's crucial to remain vigilant against scams. Be wary of any investment that promises guaranteed returns with little to no risk. Genuine passive income opportunities usually require some combination of initial investment, time, or effort.

Neglecting Your Investments: While the goal is to generate income passively, this doesn't mean you can ignore your investments entirely. Regular monitoring and management are necessary to ensure they continue to perform well. This might involve adjusting your strategies, reinvesting profits, or even cutting losses when necessary.

Letting Fear Hold You Back: Fear of failure is a common obstacle that prevents many from pursuing their passive income goals. Remember that risk is an inherent part of any investment, but it can be managed. Educate yourself, start small if you need to, and gradually build your confidence along with your portfolio.

Building a Strong Foundation

Start with What You Know: Begin your passive income journey in areas where you have some expertise or interest. This gives you a foundation of knowledge to build on and can make the process more enjoyable and engaging. As you gain experience, you can explore new avenues with confidence.

Automate and Outsource: As your passive income streams grow, look for opportunities to automate processes and outsource tasks. This can free up your time and allow you to focus on scaling your investments or exploring new opportunities. Tools like automated investment platforms, virtual assistants, and property management services can be invaluable.

Maintain Financial Discipline: The financial discipline involves both managing your investments wisely and keeping personal expenditures in check. Avoid lifestyle inflation, where increased income leads to increased spending, thereby negating the benefits of your passive income. Instead, focus on saving and investing to build wealth over time.

Set Realistic Expectations: It's important to have realistic expectations about the potential returns from your passive income streams. While some investments can yield high returns, others might offer more modest but steady income. Understand the potential of each investment and set your expectations accordingly.

Stay Patient and Persistent: Building a substantial passive income takes time. Patience and persistence are vital as you work to establish and grow your income streams. Celebrate small victories along the way, and don't be discouraged by setbacks.

With time and effort, your passive income can provide the financial freedom and security you desire.

In conclusion, while the journey towards creating successful passive income streams is filled with challenges, the rewards of financial independence and flexibility are well within reach. By applying the strategies and insights shared in this chapter, you can navigate the common pitfalls and position yourself for success. Remember, the key to building and sustaining passive income lies in continuous learning, diligent planning, and unwavering perseverance.

Summary Chapter: Venturing on Your Passive Income Journey

As we conclude our exploration of "101 Passive Income Ideas: Unlocking Financial Freedom," it's essential to reflect on the journey we've embarked upon together. This book has not only introduced you to a myriad of passive income streams but has also equipped you with the knowledge and tools necessary to begin building a future of financial independence and security.

Key Takeaways:

1. **Diverse Opportunities**: We've delved into various categories, from online ventures and real estate investments to creative pursuits and entrepreneurial efforts. The diversity of options ensures that there is something for everyone, regardless of your interests, skills, or initial investment capabilities.

2. **Foundational Knowledge**: Understanding the concept of passive income and recognizing the difference between passive and active income is crucial. This foundation has set the stage for you to evaluate and pursue opportunities with a clear understanding of their potential to generate sustained earnings.

3. **Actionable Steps**: Each chapter provided actionable advice, from starting a blog or YouTube channel to investing in real estate or financial products. The detailed step-by-step guides aim to demystify the process of initiating and growing your passive income streams.

4. **Realistic Perspectives**: While the allure of passive income is strong, we've also discussed the challenges and considerations. Acknowledging these realities ensures that you embark on this journey with a balanced view, prepared to tackle obstacles and adapt to changes.

5. **The Importance of Diversification**: Building a diversified portfolio of passive income streams can optimize your earnings and spread risk. This strategy is key to achieving long-term financial stability and growth.

6. **Patience and Persistence**: The journey to building significant passive income is neither quick nor easy. Success requires patience, persistence, and a willingness to learn and adapt over time.

Moving Forward:

As you move forward, remember that the journey to financial freedom is personal and unique. What works for one individual may not work for another. Therefore, it's important to:

- **Start Small**: Begin with one or two ideas that resonate with you and require an investment (time, effort, or money) you're comfortable with.

- **Learn and Adapt**: Be open to learning from both successes and failures. The landscape of passive income is ever-evolving, and flexibility is key.

- **Stay Motivated**: Keep your financial goals in mind. There will be challenges, but the potential rewards of financial independence and the ability to live on your own terms are immeasurable.

Conclusion:

"101 Passive Income Ideas: Unlocking Financial Freedom" is more than just a book; it's a guide to transforming your financial future. The path to passive income is diverse, allowing for creativity and innovation. Whether you're drawn to online businesses, real estate, creative endeavors, or financial investments, the opportunities are vast and varied. By taking action on the ideas that most resonate with you and committing to continuous learning and adaptation, you can build a portfolio of passive income streams that not only sustains but also enriches your life.

Embark on this journey with confidence, knowing that each step you take brings you closer to the ultimate goal of financial freedom. The road may be long, and the effort required may be significant, but the rewards of achieving passive income are well worth the pursuit.

www.ingramcontent.com/pod-product-compliance
Lightning Source LLC
Chambersburg PA
CBHW070837290526
45795CB00002B/895